EXAMPLES *from* THIS BOOK

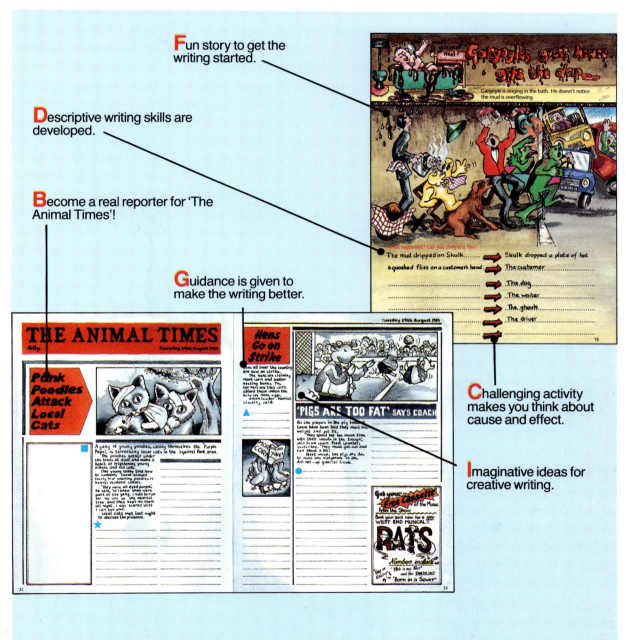

Fun story to get the writing started.

Descriptive writing skills are developed.

Become a real reporter for 'The Animal Times'!

Guidance is given to make the writing better.

Challenging activity makes you think about cause and effect.

Imaginative ideas for creative writing.

IN *this*

*T*he entire process of writing – for life – has one very practical purpose: communication. All writing is for communication.

In Writing 1, activities are used to develop different types of written communication – writing letters, creative story writing, making lists and notes, writing poems and so on.

As part of these activities and as separate ones too, we also improve skills in three vital areas.

SPELLING & VOCABULARY

Poor spelling can make a bad impression and make communication difficult.

Reading a wide range of books can help a lot. So will the spelling activities in this book and the Success! Practice books.

But it's also vital to encourage the growth of a rich vocabulary. Give your child the **confidence to try out new words – talk about different ways of saying things, and repeat new words once or twice so the child gets the hang of them.**

Among others these activities will help:

A tricky wordsearch on page 22 involves a number of words which are often spelt incorrectly. Attention is drawn to the most common errors, with encouragement to write the words carefully and correctly. This is not a dreary copying exercise, but takes the form of a wordsearch which most children will enjoy.

The Topsy Turvy crossword on pages 16 and 27 is an exercise in thinking about the opposites of simple words in order to solve a puzzle.

BOOK

Handwriting.

Legible writing is important – your child can't communicate ideas if the writing can't be read. Also neat handwriting tends to get higher marks in exams! These are some of the activities that will help:

The nosey teacher on page 8 encourages an awareness of different styles of handwriting and suggests writing in different ways so that you can compare the results together.

Alphabet soup on page 26, apart from being a reminder about alphabetical order, also gives you an opportunity to check how your child writes every single letter of the alphabet in the context of a sentence.

What's for tea? on page 36 looks like a puzzle and draws attention to a particular aspect of handwriting that some children find difficult – ascenders (d, h, l, t) and descenders (g, j, y).

66 GRAMMAR! 99

This is a basic understanding of the way in which words work together, so it is about parts of speech and grammatical rules, punctuation, sentence construction and so on.

Activities like these encourage thinking about the way our language works. This will make your child's writing better.

Tatty Tricia and Sid Genius on page 14 contains a number of very common spelling and grammatical errors to spot and correct. Sid Genius gives all the right answers as usual! Can your child find all the errors? Are there any that cause particular problems?

Super Titch and the Gorilla on page 38 is a puzzle based around the idea of nouns, and the activity is designed to increase awareness of how words function. You could (gently) draw attention to Sid Genius' comment at the bottom of the page.

Too many guests at Gargoyle's Guest House on page 44 looks really revolting and is designed for practising some tricky plurals (e.g. tomatoes, loaves).

HOW THIS BOOK *works*

Y ou can share in the fun of **Success!** If you want, you can do some of the activities with your child. But **Success!** does not depend on you. One of the benefits of the range is to encourage children to enjoy working independently, not just when the grown-ups are around.

YOU

have a special role to play. It's the one that comes naturally to any parent: give all the encouragement you can!

If you can give your child the benefits of more individual attention, there is no need for you to *teach* specific skills. **Success!** does not require specialist knowledge.

WHEN

you're ready to start on this book at home, sit down together and go through it. Talk about the activities and the zany characters, and enjoy the often crazy situations. Start one or two activities to get the feel of them.

Then, help to choose an activity to be completed and say that you'd like to see it when it's done.

HOW

will you know things are going well? When your child is absorbed, *thinking* about the activity and really *doing* the work, then you'll know that progress is being made. Look at the back of this book for further guidance.

Speed isn't important. Enjoyment and commitment are the telling signs.

WHAT

should your response be? Praise the results – don't criticise. If you think there is a better way of doing something, suggest it as an alternative, not as the only right way.

Make it clear that working at the activities is a good thing which brings praise. Effort does deserve recognition and it *will* bring results. Not least important, it will give confidence and increase enthusiasm for more activities and more learning.

Look out for opportunities to encourage work on other activities but go for short, frequent sessions – don't let it get boring!

Don't forget to *tick* off each completed activity on the *contents* page and share the sense of achievement and pleasure.

Success! Contents

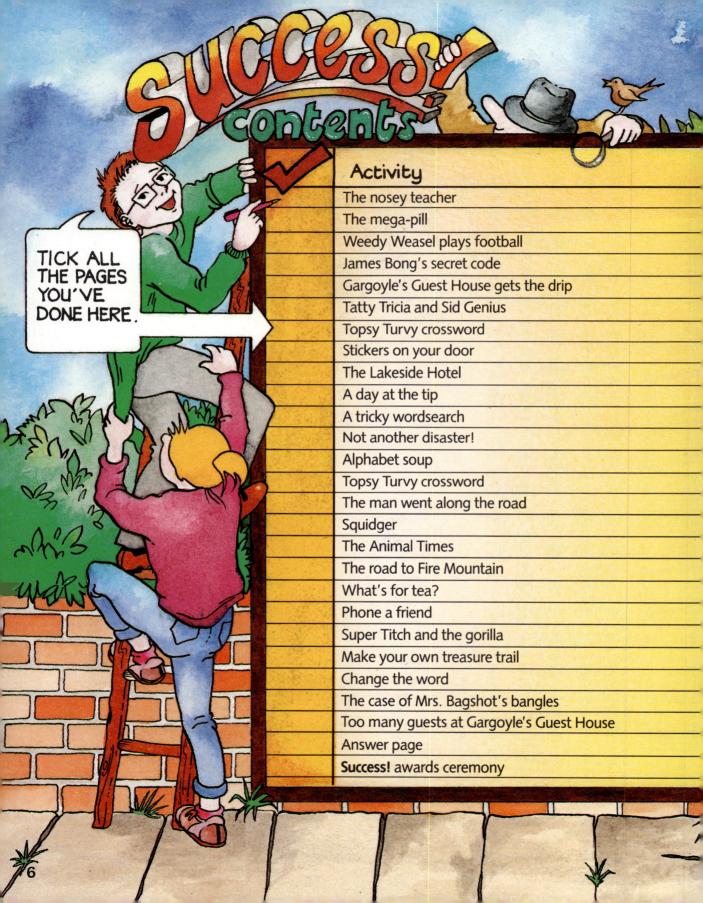

TICK ALL THE PAGES YOU'VE DONE HERE.

Writing Skills

THE NOSEY TEACHER

Do you like limericks?
Here is a limerick for you to read.

What's a limerick, Sid?

Read this one and you'll see, stupid!

There was a young teacher from Harrow,
Whose nose was too long and too narrow.
It gave so much trouble,
That he bent it up double,
And wheeled it round school in a barrow.

What do you think of the limerick?

Write here

excellent! awful! dreadful! Quite good! horrible marvellous! not bad!

........marrelous........

....

....

Copy out this limerick on a piece of paper

⭐ in your best handwriting
⭐ then in your ordinary handwriting
⭐ then as quickly as you can
★ then with your other hand.

I'll do it with my eyes closed!

Look at what I've done!

That looks like your best handwriting!

There was a young teacher from Harrow

What do you think of your handwriting?

⭐ My best handwriting is ....

⭐ My ordinary handwriting is ....

⭐ My quick handwriting is ....

★ My writing with my other hand is ....

8

You have found a bottle hidden in a secret place. It is very old. On it in old writing are the words THE MEGA-PILL. Inside it is a big green pill and on the pill are the words EAT ME. You know you should not eat it (how many times have you been told not to touch pills in bottles?). But somehow you cannot help yourself, the pill looks so tempting. You slip it into your mouth. Soon you begin to grow and grow and GROW. Every day you are much bigger than you were before. You write down each day how big you become. Like this:

THE MEGA-PILL

On the first day I was as big as
    I always am.
On the second day I grew as tall as
    our front door.
On the third day I grew so big
    I could see into my neighbour's bedroom.
On the fourth day I was high enough to
    fix the aerial on our roof.

On the fifth day I was ....

....

On the sixth day ....

....

On the seventh day ....

....

Can you complete the poem? How big will you become? Will you reach into outer space? You could try to go as far as ten days, or even more, but you'll need a separate piece of paper if you do this.

Look how well I played football on Saturday! Hey, they've left out all the things I said. I can't write them in, I'm too tired! Can you do it? You'd better write *neatly* because you've got to keep all the words in the bubbles!

Wee

Oh bore! Saturday again. .... must get a hobby.

let's Play.

oh no!!...

Come on. We're late.

Grrr! Where's the goalkeeper?

What do I have to do!

Just stop the balls.

ahhh

Well Stopped!

y Weasel plays football

James Bong's Secret Code

HFU PVU PG UIF XBZ

I wonder what this says. It's in my special code. It must be from N.

You can find out what's in the message for James Bong. You can use his secret code to write messages to your friends. Here's what you do.

Copy out the alphabet, then write it out again underneath, in CAPITAL letters, but this time start with B instead of A. We've done a few for you.

a b c d e f g h i j k l m n o p q r s t u v w x y z

B C D E _ _ _ _ _ _ K _ _ _ _ _ _ R _ _ _ _ _ X _ _ A

UIJT JT GVO!

The small letters on the top row are for real words. The **CAPITAL LETTERS** on the bottom row are for **CODE WORDS.**

So if you want to write 'help' you'd write **IFMQ** instead.

What did James Bong's message say?

Now you can read the code and send secret messages. What does this message say?

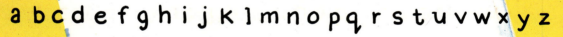

UVSO UP QBHF GPSUZ - TJY

Gargoyle's guest house gets the drip

Gargoyle is singing in the bath. He doesn't notice the mud is overflowing.

What happened? Can you complete this?

The mud dripped on Skulk........ ➡ Skulk dropped a plate of hot

squashed flies on a customer's head. ➡ The customer ....

.... ➡ The dog ....

.... ➡ The waiter ....

.... ➡ The ghouls ....

.... ➡ The driver ....

.... ➡ ....

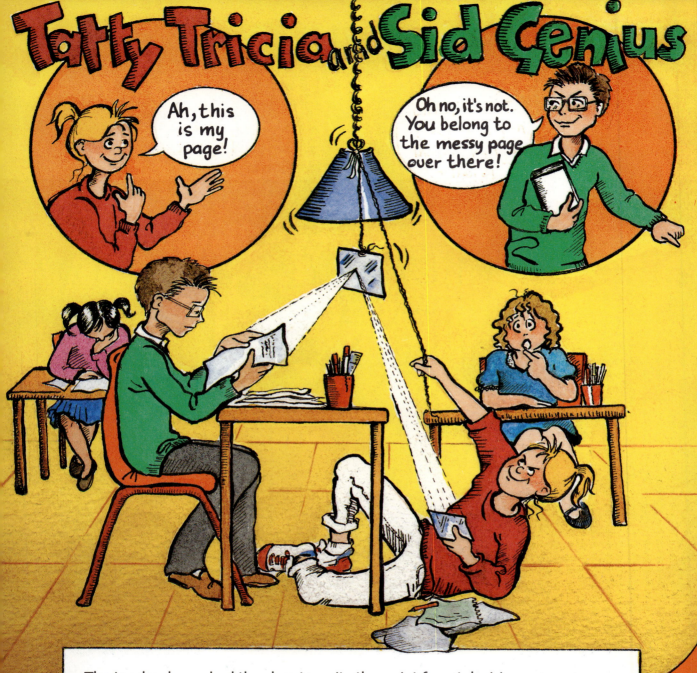

The teacher has asked the class to write the script for a television news programme.

Sid had no problems. He wrote this.

Tatty Tricia couldn't think what to write so she tried to copy Sid. This is what she wrote.

Can you be teacher and mark Tatty Tricia's work? Use a red pen and write the correct words or capital letters underneath her mistakes. Then give her a mark out of ten. You might want to make a comment!

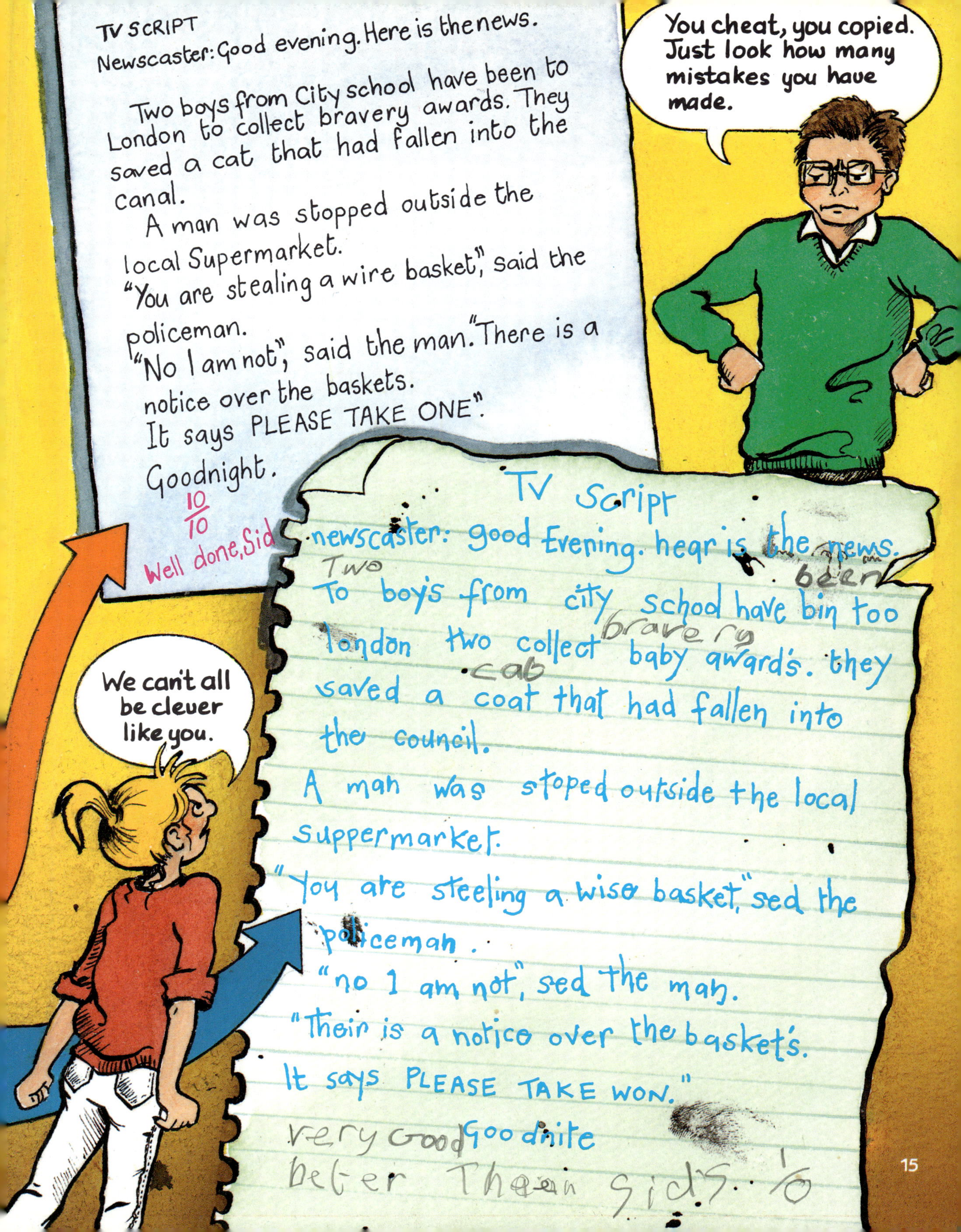
TV SCRIPT
Newscaster: Good evening. Here is the news.
Two boys from City school have been to London to collect bravery awards. They saved a cat that had fallen into the canal.
A man was stopped outside the local Supermarket.
"You are stealing a wire basket," said the policeman.
"No I am not," said the man. "There is a notice over the baskets.
It says PLEASE TAKE ONE".
Goodnight.
10/10
Well done, Sid
You cheat, you copied. Just look how many mistakes you have made.
We can't all be clever like you.
TV Script
newscaster: good Evening. hear is the news.
Two
To boys from city school have bin too
been
bravery
london two collect baby award's. they
cab
saved a coat that had fallen into the council.
A man was stoped outside the local suppermarket.
"You are steeling a wise basket," sed the policeman.
"no I am not," sed the man.
"Their is a notice over the basket's.
It says PLEASE TAKE WON."
Goodnite
very Good
beter Than Sid's. 1/0

Stickers on your door

What does your bedroom door look like?
Would you like to put stickers on it?
Check with your parents first! What about these?

You can try some out here first.

This is Skulk's bedroom door. What stickers do you think he has on his door?
Write them in.

The Lakeside Hotel

Jack and Norah welcome you to the Lakeside Hotel.

If you are looking for an escape from it all, this is the place for you! We are miles away from the nearest town.

We don't have:

- music
- a television
- video games

We do have:

- good, home cooked food
- comfortable bedrooms
- peace and quiet

Lakeside Hotel
Sunshine Lane
Warmington
Sundown
Tel (0998) 634 5789

Enjoy long country walks! Enjoy fishing on the lake (we have a boat you can use). Or just relax in our beautiful garden and watch the many lovely birds.

Our guests usually like to go to bed early, so our small bar closes at 9 p.m. and we ask people not to make any noise after that time.

You'll want to come back!

Here are some of the guests at the hotel.

John and his parents are spending their first holiday here. He and his father spend most days fishing on the lake. His mother reads a lot and jogs around the lake early in the morning. They play 'Scrabble' in the evenings.

Hester and her husband come here every year. They are artists and spend a lot of time painting. They also go for long walks and watch the animals and birds.

Steve has brought his elderly mother here. She has come before but it is his first time. She spends her days sitting in the garden, reading and sleeping. Steve drives off to the town in his fast car whenever he can. His mother makes him spend the evenings playing cards with her.

These three people all started to write postcards to their friends. Can you guess which of them has started which card? Can you finish off the postcards? Make up a name and address for each card. What do you think each of them says about the hotel? What do they say about the way they spend their time?

1 August

It's so peaceful here! Saw some lovely deer yesterday

1st Aug

Aaaargh! This place is TERRIBLE!

1st Aug

I thought it was really going to be boring here, but it's great

A day at the tip

MAKE A LIST

Skulk and Gargoyle are looking for things for their new house.

Make a list of all the things they can take, putting each into the right room. We've done two for you.

Living room
telephone

Bathroom

Bedroom
Draws
Bed
mirra

Kitchen
Spoon
Plate
Cooker

Garden shed
wheelbarrow
rake

A TRICKY WORDSEARCH

This is a wordsearch for you to make. You can then try it out on somebody else.

The tricky bit is that you will use words which people often spell wrongly.

friend   beautiful   horrible   February
writing   straight   dining room   bicycle
Wednesday   biscuit   excited   terrible

The letters in red show where people sometimes get the word wrong. So look carefully before you write them in. You'll have to write the letters carefully too. We've put two words in for you.

When you've put all the words in, fill up the other squares with any letters you like. Then try it out on somebody. You'll need to give the person a list of the words you have hidden in your wordsearch.

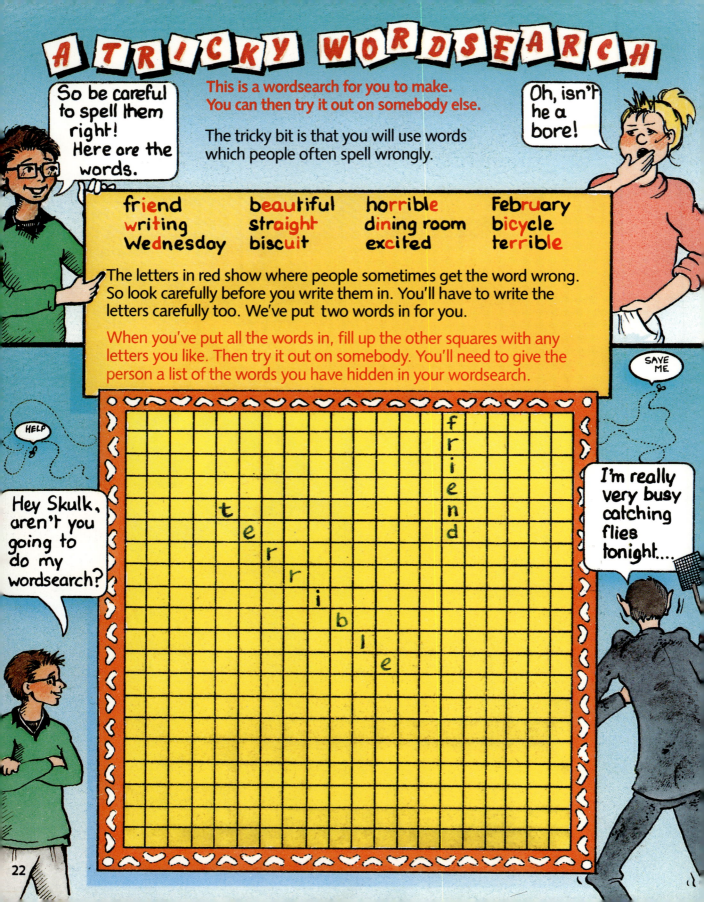

22

Not another disaster!

On the next two pages is a board game you can finish off and play. You don't need to pull the pages out of the book to play the game.

You do need to finish making the game!

Each red square on the board shows something happening which makes the journey more difficult. We have filled in two squares for you.

What else could happen?

Something could go wrong with the car?

Something terrible could happen at the river?

The pictures may give you more ideas.

Car could blow up!

BOOM!

MONSTER!

I've left all my money in the cafe!

TIGER! eating sandwiches

Write your ideas of what could happen in the red squares.

The green squares show when something happens which makes the journey more pleasant. We have filled in two for you.

What else could happen?

The car could develop magical powers?

The weather could really help you along?

The pictures may give you more ideas.

Magic!

The only way to travel!

Let's all have a drink!

Write your ideas of what could happen in the green squares.

Now you need a counter or button for each player, a dice, and someone to play with. You don't need to get the exact number at the end to win.

Who wrote this book? Don't they know that DICE is the plural? It should be die.

Is someone going to die?

NOW PLAY THE GAME!

23

25

Alphabet Soup!

That's nonsense!

Every modern queen has a pretty box of jolly brown socks which she keeps for her lazy husband the king.

If you look carefully you can see that every letter of the alphabet is used in this sentence.

See if you can make up a sentence using all the letters of the alphabet. Try it on a piece of paper first before you write it here. Cross out the letters in the bowl as you use them.

Write your sentence here.

I don't fancy this soup. There are no slugs in it.

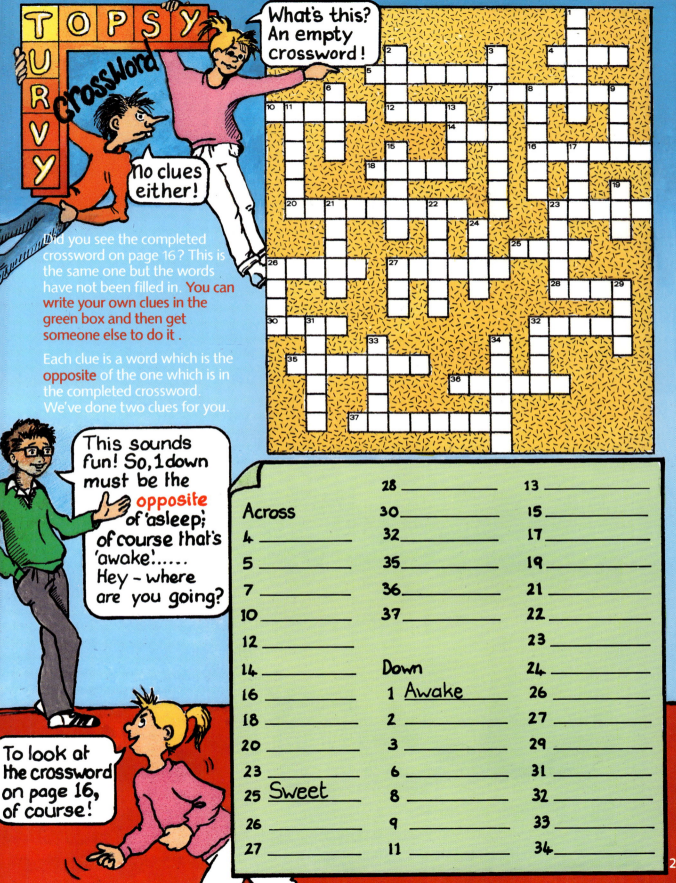

The man went along the road...

Here are three pictures. 'The man went along the road' could describe any of them.

The man walked st
more steps, then fell
He raised his head pa
along the dusty roa

Let's make it more interesting.
For instance, start by giving the man a name.
What did he look like? (e.g. he was dressed in. . . . he looked . . .)
How did he go along the road? (e.g. staggered, crawled, ran . . .)
What was the road like?
What could he see?
Why was he there?
What happens next?

Pick one of the pictures and write down the answers to some of these questions on a separate piece of paper.

You needn't answer all of the questions. You don't need to answer them in the same order. You can put in extra bits of your own.

You might try doing a rough version first, just jotting down a few words. Then you can try writing it as a proper story.

We've started a rough version for one of the pictures. If you like you could base your story on our notes or do your own. It's your story!

Now you can use your ideas to start your story. Ours might start like this. How do you want to start your story?

You can do the same things when you have to write a story at school!

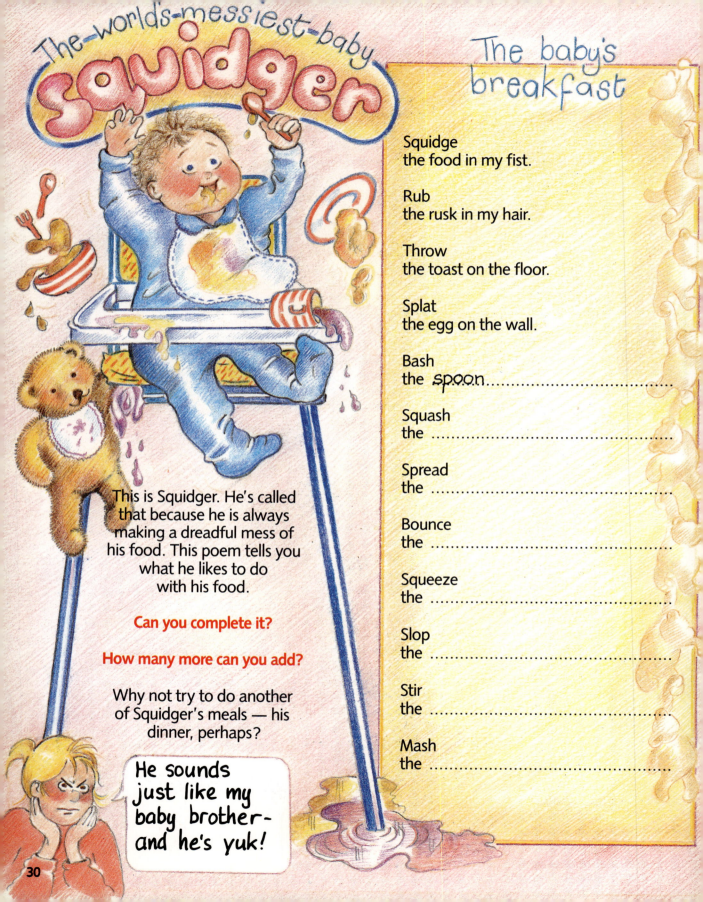

The world's messiest baby
Squidger

The baby's breakfast

Squidge
the food in my fist.

Rub
the rusk in my hair.

Throw
the toast on the floor.

Splat
the egg on the wall.

Bash
the *spoon*..............................

Squash
the ....

Spread
the ....

Bounce
the ....

Squeeze
the ....

Slop
the ....

Stir
the ....

Mash
the ....

This is Squidger. He's called that because he is always making a dreadful mess of his food. This poem tells you what he likes to do with his food.

Can you complete it?

How many more can you add?

Why not try to do another of Squidger's meals — his dinner, perhaps?

He sounds just like my baby brother- and he's yuk!

30

THE ANIMAL TIMES

Hey look, there's a newspaper on the next page.

But it isn't finished.

Can you finish the stories? The questions will help you. You need to put in captions for the photographs as well.

This sounds like hard work . . . .

Punk poodles attack local cats ★

What happened at the meeting?

Who spoke?

What did the cats decide to do?

Did the reporter manage to interview a Purple Pup?

If so, what did he say about the gang?

Pigs are too fat ●

Tell the readers something about the kangaroo team.

Do they have a good record?

Who have they beaten so far?

Who is their best player?

What does their captain say about their chances of beating the pigs?

Hens go on strike ▲

What did the Union leader say?

What did the striking hens say to the reporter?

What did the farmers say?

Is there any chance of an agreement?

Do the hens have any other complaints they'd like to see put right?

Try out another advert. ■

You could do one on comfortable cat baskets, tuneful cow bells, heated dog beds, or for property like luxury hen houses, modern cowsheds. . . .

Over

THE ANIMAL TIMES

40p

Tuesday 29th August 1989

Punk Poodles Attack Local Cats

A gang of young poodles, calling themselves the 'Purple Pups', is terrorising local cats in the Squirrel Park area.

The poodles gather under the trees at dusk and make a habit of frightening young kittens and old cats.

One young tabby told how he suddenly found himself facing four snarling poodles in heavy, studded collars.

'They were all dyed purple', he said, 'So I knew they were part of the gang. I had to run for my life up the nearest tree and they kept me there all night. I was scared stiff I can tell you'.

Local cats met last night to discuss the problem.

Hens Go on Strike

Hens all over the country are now on strike.

The hens are claiming more corn and better nesting boxes. The farmers say they can't afford these unless the hens lay more eggs.

Union leader Harriet Clucking said:

▲ _____
_____
_____
_____

'PIGS ARE TOO FAT' SAYS COACH

All the players in the pig football team have been told they must lose weight and get fit.

'They spend far too much time with their snouts in the trough', said team coach Fred Grunter, yesterday. 'They must get out and run about a bit.'

Next week, the pigs are due to meet the Kangaroos in the Animal Cup quarter finals.

● _____
_____
_____

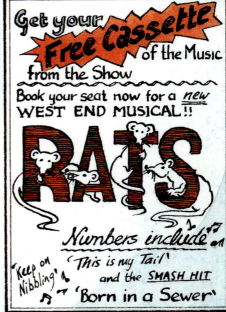

Time is running out for Ehad. He is held captive at the bottom of Fire Mountain by the evil Boron. Boron has set the automatic lava flow to begin one hour before sunset. Will Ehad be burnt alive? Can Dara reach him in time? You have the map. You must write careful instructions for Dara.

One false step and she will fall victim to Boron's Swamp men or one of the many dangers that lurk on the road to Fire Mountain. There is only one safe path.

Write your instructions on a separate piece of paper. You could start like this. Turn left between Vampire wood and Devil's lagoon. Then turn first right between the snake pits. Watch out for the snakes.

The road to Fir

Falling rocks!

Ha
ro

Snake pit

VAMPIRE wood

Devil's lagoon

Black tower

Dara

Swamp man

start

But I can't read these words. Gargoyle has been sticking tape over them.

Can you guess what these words are?

What's for tea?

jelly

I've done one for you. Can you write in the others?

Some letters have tall lines that go up. These are ascenders.

Some letters have lines that go down below the line. These are descenders.

b d f h k l t   g j p q y

Ascenders and descenders are **important**. They help people to read your writing.

When you are writing in lines make sure the ascenders touch the top line and that the descenders touch the bottom line.

Now what's Gargoyle doing?

Gargoyle put the fat lady in the fridge

Now write your own sentence here. See how many ascenders and descenders you can use. You can use the words that we have used or use your own.

Here is half a phone conversation. You are phoning your friend. We've written what you said, but what do you think your friend said? Write in the gaps. We've written it like a play, so there's no need for speech marks.

You: Hi, it's me! Are you going into town this afternoon?

Friend: ....

You: But why can't you?

Friend: ....

....

You: Oh, I see. How long has she been ill?

Friend: ....

You: Have you taken her to the vet?

Friend: ....

....

You: Well, I think you should.

Friend: ....

You: We've got a big cardboard box you could use.

Friend: ....

You: O.K. I'll bring it round to your house about two o'clock. Bye.

This is Tina Trouble

And this is SUPER TITCH!

Fill in the gaps and learn of my terrible adventure. We've done three for you.

Super Titch and The Gorilla

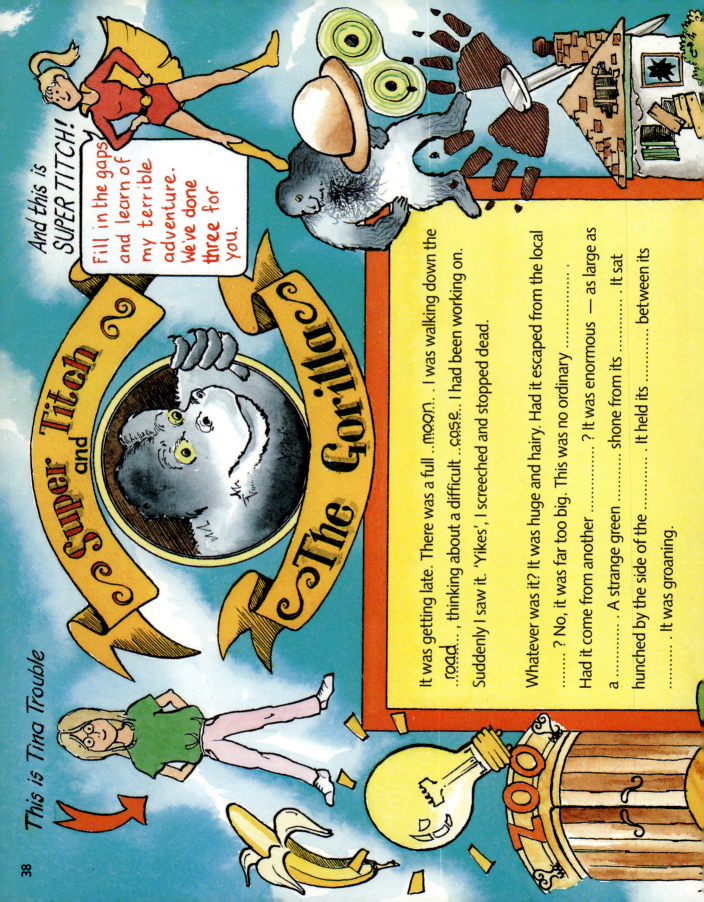

It was getting late. There was a full ..moon.. . I was walking down the ..road.. , thinking about a difficult ..case.. . I had been working on.

Suddenly I saw it. 'Yikes', I screeched and stopped dead.

Whatever was it? It was huge and hairy. Had it escaped from the local ....? No, it was far too big. This was no ordinary .... Had it come from another .... ? It was enormous — as large as a .... A strange green .... shone from its .... It sat hunched by the side of the .... It held its .... between its .... It was groaning.

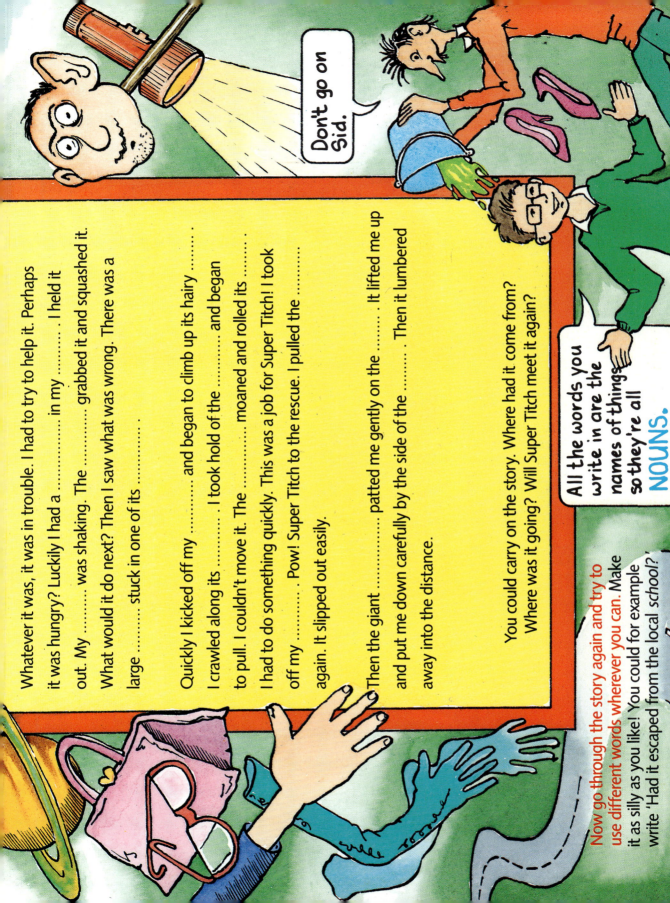

Whatever it was, it was in trouble. I had to try to help it. Perhaps it was hungry? Luckily I had a .... in my .... I held it out. My .... was shaking. The .... grabbed it and squashed it. What would it do next? Then I saw what was wrong. There was a large .... stuck in one of its ....

Quickly I kicked off my .... and began to climb up its hairy .... I crawled along its .... I took hold of the .... and began to pull. I couldn't move it. The .... moaned and rolled its .... I had to do something quickly. This was a job for Super Titch! I took off my .... Pow! Super Titch to the rescue. I pulled the .... again. It slipped out easily.

Then the giant .... patted me gently on the .... It lifted me up and put me down carefully by the side of the .... Then it lumbered away into the distance.

You could carry on the story. Where had it come from? Where was it going? Will Super Titch meet it again?

Don't go on Sid.

All the words you write in are the names of things so they're all NOUNS.

Now go through the story again and try to use different words wherever you can. Make it as silly as you like! You could for example write 'Had it escaped from the local *school?*'

39

Write your clues on nine bits of paper. We've written the first three and the last one for you.

Give this first clue to a friend — it will tell them where to look for the next clue.

Make your own Treasure Trail

Hide Clue 2 near the bath.

3. Look for the next clue where everyone wipes their feet.

1. You will find the next clue where you can have a good soak.

2. Find the next clue near something you need if you want a good fry up.

Hide Clue 3 under a frying pan.

Hide Clue 4 under the doormat.

4. Make your own clue for looking near the telephone.

Hide Clue 6 near the washing-up liquid.

5. Make your own clue for looking near the washing-up liquid.

6. Make your own clue for looking in the settee.

Hide Clue 5 near the telephone.

Hide Clue 7 in the settee.

Hide Clue 8 near the bookshelf.

Hide Clue 9 near the television.

Hide the treasure in the fridge.

7. Make your own clue for looking on the bookshelf.

8. Make your own clue for looking near the television.

9. Nearly there! You will find the treasure where it's really cold.

40

CHANGE THE WORD

How can you turn the word 'dog' into the word 'rub', changing only one letter at a time?

Like this: dog   dug   rug   rub

Or you could take much longer, like this:

dog   dig   pig   big   bog   hog   hug   rug   rub

> Hail and Thunder Stench and Slime!.. I can't even change this dog into a pig!

Choose a word to start with...

See how many other words you can make, changing only one letter at a time.

Here are some words to start with:

dog   lid   hug   den   big   had   cod

You could play this with someone else. Take turns to change the word.

How long can you keep going?

You could make a flip book.

Choose a word to start with.
Make your list of words you can make,
changing only one letter at a time.
Get a few pieces of paper.
Fold them, like this.

> I get it! I think I'll try it out on Weedy Weasel.

1 Sew or staple along here. Cut through all the pages to make 3 sections. Then write the first word.

2 (i is underneath)

3 (p is underneath)

4 And so on . . .

Mrs. Bagshot's jewellery has been stolen. The pictures show her bedroom before and after the crime. Inspector Brain is making notes about the clues which may help him find the villain. He has written the first one. Can you see any other clues? **Write your notes in the Inspector's notebook.**

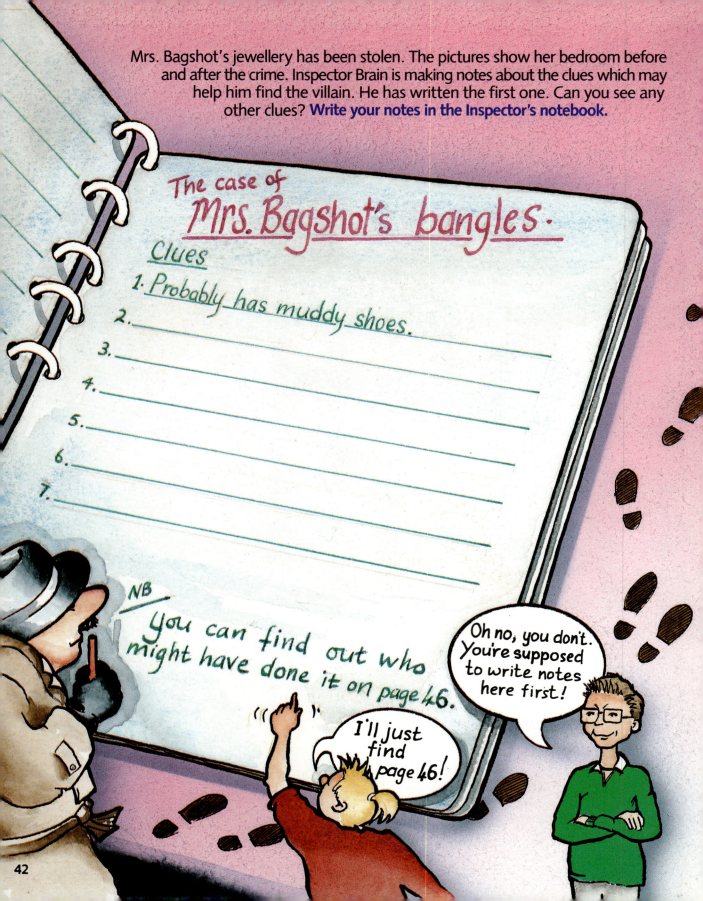

Before the crime

After the crime

Gargoyle's spell makes lots more of everything.
Here is Skulk's list. Can you fill in the gaps? We've done the first one for you.

61 devilled _____flies_____ on toast

100 _____ of stewed slugs

72 barbecued _____

600 smoked adder _____

1000 rotten _____

500 stuffed _____

60 _____ of green bog water

59 toadspawn _____ and slime

25 _____ with maggot sauce

45 _____ of shredded worms

56 mouldy _____

96 pickled _____

Can you spell too?
Turn to page 46
for the answers.

45

ANSWER PAGE

Did you put all these in the right place?

Too many guests at Gargoyle's Guest House

Here are the answers

flies sandwiches peaches
dishes tomatoes boxes
mice cockroaches loaves
glasses woodlice
jellies

If you've got them all right I'll send you a special box of stewed slugs.

A day at the tip

Living Room — telephone, lamp, cushion, settee, armchair, carpet, radio, pot plant

Bathroom — bath, sink, toy duck, razor, back scratcher, mirror, toothbrush

Bedroom — bed, blanket, wardrobe, alarm clock, chest of drawers, mattress

Kitchen — saucepan, kettle, cooker, fridge, broom, spoon, plate

Garden Shed — wheelbarrow, bicycle, lawn mower, deck chair, hose, garden fork, watering can, hammer, paint, ladder, saw

Mrs. Bagshot's bangles

Did you note all the clues?

wears glasses
has a cold
likes watching television
smokes cigars
wears a striped suit
wears a rose in his buttonhole
likes chocolates
has muddy shoes

James Bong's Secret Code

XFMM EPOF!

46

And now – ladies and gentlemen. The success awards ceremony!

the Success! AWARDS CEREMONY

Be the judge and give these famous awards to the pages you thought were best. Write in the names of the activities you choose on the lines.

I give the TATTY TRICIA PONY TAIL AWARD to the activity I enjoyed most.

This was ....

I give the SID GENIUS SPECTACLES AWARD to the activity I did best.

This was ....

I give the WEEDY WEASEL TEETH AWARD to the activity I thought was the funniest.

This was ....

But I give the SKULK DEAD RAT AWARD to the activity I thought was the worst.

This was ....

I didn't like this one because ....

Try to give a reason. Was it really boring? Was it not funny? Was it too hard?

SUCCESS!

means GREAT IDEAS

66 *The very best educational process lies in a confident partnership between child, parents and teachers.* **99**

Success! gives you the chance to make your contribution as effective as possible. We provide a range of imaginative opportunities for you to select from. They can be combined in different ways to achieve the progress you are looking for.

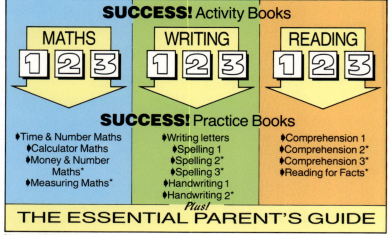

SUCCESS! Activity Books

| MATHS | WRITING | READING |
| 1 2 3 | 1 2 3 | 1 2 3 |

SUCCESS! Practice Books

- ◆ Time & Number Maths
- ◆ Calculator Maths
- ◆ Money & Number Maths*
- ◆ Measuring Maths*

- ◆ Writing letters
- ◆ Spelling 1
- ◆ Spelling 2*
- ◆ Spelling 3*
- ◆ Handwriting 1
- ◆ Handwriting 2*

- ◆ Comprehension 1
- ◆ Comprehension 2*
- ◆ Comprehension 3*
- ◆ Reading for Facts*

Plus!
THE ESSENTIAL PARENT'S GUIDE

* in preparation

SUCCESS! *activity books*

This book is only one of nine activity books covering Maths, Writing and Reading. These books provide challenging and attractive exercises in the *whole business* of the main subjects.
You can choose the subject or subjects that you think particularly need help, and start with the first Level in each one to see how much progress can be made.

SUCCESS! *practice books*

This is a series of books designed to improve specific skills which are part of the whole business of each subject. The exercises are easier than the Activity Books, but they are still lots of fun to do. They concentrate on building ability and confidence in the basic tools everyone needs to be good at the subjects.